Bill Colombi

Mathematics and Computers

Illustrated by Graham Cooke

Wayland

Endeavour Books

Initiated and edited by Stella Robinson, the books in the Endeavour series have been researched and written by qualified scientists and engineers and each title covers one aspect of man's scientific and technological development.

With the help of biographical notes, full colour illustrations and explanatory diagrams, each book highlights the major personalities, discoveries and developments in a particular field of scientific or technological progress.

Ranging in scope from earliest times to the present day, the series provides a comprehensive account of man's struggle to understand the natural world and organize the environment to his benefit; man's scientific endeavour.

Other titles in the series

Buildings	Tools and Manufacturing
Engines	Iron and Steel
Farming	Resources
Health and Medicine	Textiles

First published in 1985 by Wayland (Publishers) Limited
49 Landsdowne Place, Brighton, East Sussex BN3 1HF, England
© Copyright 1985 Design Practitioners
ISBN 0 85078 347 X

Designed and Typeset by DP Press, Sevenoaks, Kent
Printed in Italy by G. Canale & C.S.p.A., Turin

Contents

From numbers to mathematics

Do you still furtively count on your fingers when your teacher asks mental arithmetic questions round the class? If you do, then having ten fingers is very handy, since our present way of counting is based on numbers from one to ten. But why stop at ten? The Sibiller tribesmen of New Guinea find twenty-seven different parts of the body to point to when indicating numbers! In this method lies the root of the problem that many people have with mathematics. When pointing to the nose these tribesmen do not mean one nose, or even fourteen noses, they are symbolizing the number 14.

People in other cultures have devised alternative ways of counting using different *base numbers*, such as five, twenty and even sixty; with each number up to the base number having a different name and symbol to represent it. Although using base ten, the decimal system, is now almost universal, other base numbers are still used. Take, for instance, the division of hours into minutes and minutes into seconds – an example of the use of base sixty. It was only in 1967 that Parliament in Britain finally agreed to do away with the old money system of twelve pennies to the shilling and twenty shillings to the pound. The French language has 'quatre-vingts' (four twenties) for eighty. Similarly man's expected life span is said to be 'three score years and ten', in the Book of Psalms in the Bible. Score in this case means twenty.

How the name and symbol given to each number up to the base number came about is not clear. More important in the progress towards mathematics, however, is the way in which they were combined to form larger numbers. The development of *position value, decimal points* and the use of zeros was a process which took many centuries to develop. It came about as a result of warfare and trading between different cultures; knowledge, language and ideas were exchanged as well as goods.

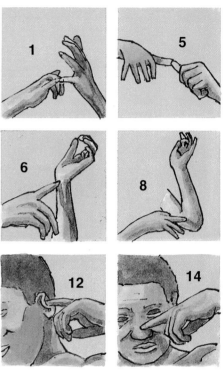

These are six examples of the signs the Sibiller tribesmen use for numbers up to 27.

We still use the base sixty when telling the time. The clock shows the time as 12:43 and 50 seconds. We are in effect saying that it is
$$12 \times 60 \times 60 + 43 \times 60 + 50$$
(= 45830) seconds past midnight, but whereas we have combined six symbols the Sumerians would only have used three, one for the hours, one for the minutes and one for the seconds.

one penny

one shilling

The weight system of pounds and ounces uses base 16. The old British system of shillings and pence used base 12.

As well as a number system, symbols have been developed to represent various mathematical operations, such as addition, subtraction, multiplication and division. As mathematics became more complicated, more and more symbols had to be introduced. As we shall see later, this has not always been an easy process. This use of symbols may make life easier for mathematicians but for many other people symbols tend to produce a mental blockage. For this reason their use has been kept to a minimum in this book.

The increasing need for record keeping in trade, accurate navigation, precise measurement in science and industry and calculation in almost every other field imaginable has called for some form of aid to arithmetic. This has been met, over the centuries, by calculating machines from the simple abacus to the modern microcomputer. The abacus works in our familiar base ten, but the computer can only count up to two before starting a new column, and can only multiply by performing repeated additions – mind you, it does do it very quickly!

As we shall see, however, the development of mathematics is not just about a science responding to a need. To many of the great mathematicians of the past the advancement of mathematics and the development of new techniques has simply been for the sheer pleasure of working with numbers – an idea some people might find hard to understand. Nevertheless, the mathematical discoveries proved useful in the end, though their practical applications might not be apparent until centuries later.

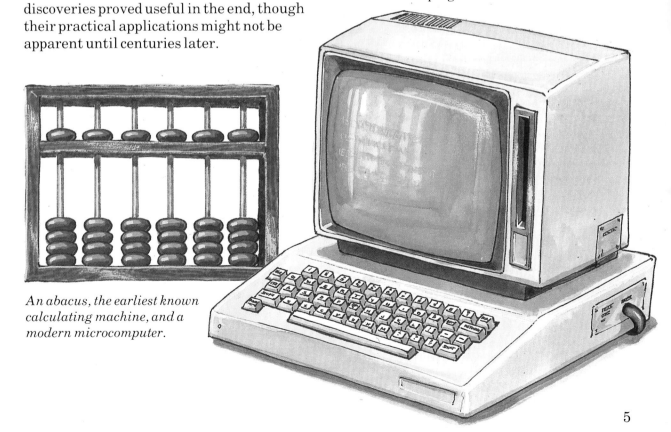

```
20:PRINT "BASE=
   10MVA"
30:INPUT "HV NE
   TWORK(MVA)="
   ;A
40:B=1000/A
45:PRINT "HV NE
   TWORK=";A;"M
   VA"
50:INPUT "HV CA
   BLE(SQ.MM)="
   ;D
55:INPUT "HV CA
   BLE LENGTH(M
   )=";P
60:INPUT "ENTER
    1 FOR AL.2
    FOR CU",C
70:IF C=1THEN 9
   0
80:IF C=2THEN 1
   30
90:E=27:H$="AL"
100:GOSUB 900
110:F=(E9*A(E+1)
    /11000^2)P
120:G=(E9*A(E+2)
    /11000^2)P:
    GOTO 140
130:E=48:H$="CU"
    :GOTO 100
140:PRINT "HV CA
    BLE=";D;"SQ.
    MM/";H$;"'S";
```

Print-out of a pocket computer program.

An abacus, the earliest known calculating machine, and a modern microcomputer.

The Bronze Age cities of the Middle East

As hunters of animals and collectors of wild fruit, early man had little need to count, measure or calculate, as long as enough food could be found to eat. However, when the hunter-gatherers turned to farming and a more settled existence in the fertile river valleys, the need for some form of number system was created.

Timing of the seasons, predictions of when rivers would flood, the measurement of food supplies and payments in trade all helped to stimulate early work on arithmetic, *algebra*, *geometry* and astronomy. In about 3000 BC the invention of bronze, an alloy of tin and copper but much harder than either, led to the replacement of stone in making tools and weapons. To achieve consistent results when making it required new skills in weighing and calculation.

Early Bronze Age tools.

One of the earliest organized civilizations grew up in Southern Mesopotamia, by the Rivers Tigris and Euphrates. Here the Sumerians built their villages and by about 3000 BC some of these villages, like Kish, Lagash and Ur had grown up into important cities. The Sumerians were a clever and inventive people; excavations show that they had four-wheeled carts and kept business and judicial records. For reasons which are not clear they used a number system based on sixty, with a different symbol for each whole number, or *integer* from one to sixty. For numbers over sixty, combinations of the integers were used just as we do today.

The Sumerians' skill in geometry is evident in their construction of irrigation systems and pyramids. They were also the first to use bricks of regular shape, not just for building walls, but also for arches and vaulted (curved) roofs.

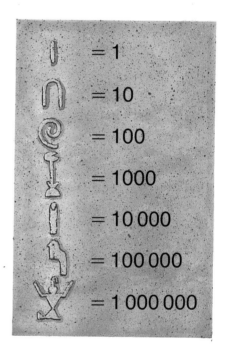

Egyptian number systems.

During this time another great civilization, that of the Egyptians, was established along the banks of the River Nile. Their number system was based on ten, but they only had a new symbol for each ten of the previous unit – thus 9 would be written with nine vertical lines, while ten was written with a new symbol (see diagram). Thus it took twenty-seven symbols to represent 999. In spite of this cumbersome system, the Egyptians made great strides forward in the use of practical geometry.

$$999 =$$

The simple decimal nine hundred and ninety-nine, compared with the same number using Egyptian symbols.

For example, the land in Egypt was divided into equal-sized plots upon which tax was paid; but when the Nile flooded each year and tore away part of the banks, the plots had to be re-surveyed to make sure that no-one paid more than their fair share. Thus skills in land surveying and the calculation of areas were well established.

The Great Pyramids are also examples of the Egyptians' skills in practical mathematics. Imagine setting out a perfect square, then building upwards at a precise angle on all four sides so as to meet at a single point over a hundred metres up. Remember that pyramids are not solid but contain intricate networks of passages and chambers, many of them secret.

As well as their skills in geometry and *trigonometry*, the Egyptians and Sumerians also had methods for calculating the areas of triangles and circles, and obtaining the volumes of various solids. The study of the stars was important to the Egyptians as a means of predicting when the Nile was about to rise and flood its banks. It happened about the time the star Sirius appeared on the horizon just before dawn.

It is believed that even at that time there were mathematicians working on problems with no practical application; but it is the rise of Greek civilization that really marks the start of mathematics as a *theoretical* subject.

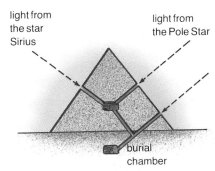

At the time the Nile was about to flood, light from Sirius shone straight down the ventilation shaft on to the face of the dead pharoah in the burial chamber.

One way of finding the height of a pyramid is to compare the length of its shadow with the length of a shadow cast by a pole of known height.

$$\frac{H}{h} = \frac{\frac{1}{2} B + S}{s}$$

$$\text{so } H = h\left(\frac{\frac{1}{2} B + S}{s}\right)$$

7

Mathematics begins with the Greek-speaking people

Before the Greeks, the Egyptians and Sumerians had made great strides in finding and using mathematical properties, for instance, that a triangle with sides of three units, four units and five units makes a perfect right-angled triangle. However, it was the Greeks, from as early as 600 BC who began to look more deeply into these practical results and produce *proofs* and general rules for these discoveries.

Thales' method for finding how far a ship is away from the shore.

SCALE 1:1000

Thales (624–546 BC), a Greek merchant from Miletus, is often referred to as the 'Father of Mathematics'. In his travels as a merchant he went to Egypt and came into contact with its mathematician monks and studied their work. As a result, when he retired early he spent his time studying philosophy, mathematics and astronomy. Besides accurately predicting the eclipse of the sun in 585 BC he devised a method for measuring the height of the Great Pyramid, gave us the correct number of days in the year and a convenient method for determining the distance away of a ship at sea. His studies covered many of the laws of geometry with which we are familiar today.

If the height of the tower is known (a), and the angles A and B at the top and bottom of the tower are measured, then a scale drawing can be made. Following the principle of similar triangles, the distance away of the ship can be measured. In this drawing the ship is about 83m from the tower.

His pupil Pythagoras (582–500 BC) also travelled widely, particularly to Egypt on Thales' advice, before setting up a school in Crotone in Southern Italy. There he lectured on philosophy and mathematics to crowds of enthusiastic listeners. Women, forbidden to go to public meetings, often broke the law to attend. Some of his pupils formed themselves into a secret society called the 'Order of the

Pythagoreans' and adopted as their symbol the star formed by the diagonals of a regular pentagon. So devoted were they to Pythagoras that all their discoveries were attributed directly to him. We cannot therefore be sure that the proof of his *theorem* was actually his own work. Pythagoras is also credited with discovering the *harmonic progression* in the notes of the musical scale, from the relationship between the length of a string and the note that it makes when it vibrates.

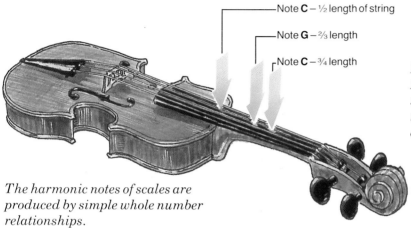

Note **C** – ½ length of string

Note **G** – ⅔ length

Note **C** – ¾ length

Pythagoras' theorem. In a right-angled triangle, the square on the hypotenuse is equal to the sum of the squares on the other two sides.

The harmonic notes of scales are produced by simple whole number relationships.

Perhaps one of the most important discoveries at the time was that of the possibility of *irrational numbers*. Until then only rational numbers (whole, or the *ratios* of whole numbers, eg 3, 8, ¾, ⅔) had been thought possible. They thought that for any two lines it must be possible to find a small unit length that would fit exactly into both lines. To the consternation of the Pythagoreans, when the diagonal of a square was measured, no suitable small unit could be found to go into the diagonal and the sides a whole number of times; no matter how small a unit was tried. It was ironic for them that when their own symbol, the star, was examined it too was found to contain irrational lengths.

This discovery was important, for not only did it upset one of their basic beliefs in whole numbers but it led Pythagoras to use a new type of indirect proof – *reductio ad absurdum* – to prove this irrationality. In this type of proof the initial assumption is taken to be correct, but as the proof is followed through the result becomes absurd and therefore the initial assumption must be incorrect. This was a very important development in the logical proof of theorems.

These early Greek-speaking mathematicians had turned mathematics into a science where now general theories could be produced and proved. The next stage was the development of mathematics as a pure science, almost completely separate from practical applications.

Pythagorean star in regular pentagon.

The length of the diagonal of the square is $\sqrt{2}$ of the length of a side. $\sqrt{2} = 1.4142135\ldots$ which is an irrational number.

The separation of theory from practice

There now followed, amongst Greek mathematicians, a tremendous surge forward in investigating mathematical ideas with thorough, or rigorous, proofs. The Greeks had a practical way of finding the area of a circle (see diagram), but to be able to prove conclusively that the answer they got was the correct answer seemed impossible. How could it be proved that the addition of an *infinite* number of infinitely small parts add up to the whole area? Zeno (490–430 BC), the leading master of the Eleatic school of philosophy, investigated the idea of infinity and how it appeared in nature.

One of the people who influenced the course of Greek thinking most was Plato (427–347 BC), who set up his Academy in Athens. Here his students were encouraged to study geometry and numbers, as he believed that a knowledge of mathematics was essential for understanding the universe; and its study the best way of training the mind. He declared that measurements, calculations and the solution of practical problems related to trade and industry were unsuitable activities for mathematicians. Plato was so devoted to geometry that he required his students to provide proofs using no more than a pair of compasses and a ruler. Plato also believed that the five regular solids (the Platonic Solids) occurred everywhere in nature, but this really came to light only with the molecular theories of today and the study of crystal structures.

Plato's narrow view severely restricted mathematical discovery for over 1500 years. Though successive generations of mathematicians began to take a somewhat broader view, new and powerful social forces prevented any major changes of outlook and practice in mathematics.

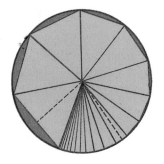

Finding the area of a circle: a circle may be divided into many small slices. The area of each slice is approximately the area of a triangle drawn within the slice. The narrower the slice the smaller the area not covered by the triangle (in dark blue). Thus the area of the circle could be calculated as approximately the sum of the areas of the triangles. If there are an infinite number of infinitely small slices then the height of the triangles will become the radius of the circle (shown by the dotted lines), and the sum of the lengths of the bases of the triangles will be the circumference of the circle. The Greeks deduced that the equation for the area of a triangle (½ base × height) could therefore be applied to the area of a circle (½ circumference × radius).

The Platonic solids

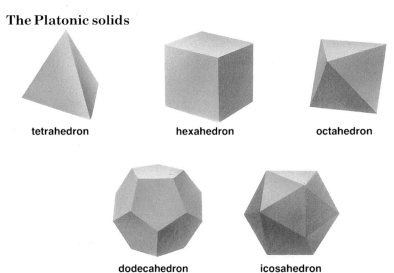

tetrahedron   hexahedron   octahedron

dodecahedron   icosahedron

Crystals of pyrites (known as fool's gold), found as a series of cubes or hexahedrons.

Alexandria: the new centre of learning

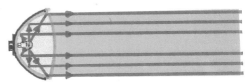

The development of mathematics shifted from Greece to North Africa when Alexander the Great (356–323 BC) conquered Greece, Egypt and the Persian Empire, towards the end of the 4th century BC. His great city, Alexandria, was a convenient meeting place for Greeks, Arabs and Jews, drawing together all the learning of the ancient world. Libraries were set up, housing the works of the leading philosophers and mathematicians of the different cultures. This intellectual centre was to last some 900 years before it was finally taken by Moslem invaders in AD 643. A great library, said to hold 700 000 volumes, was destroyed.

It was at Alexandria that Euclid taught mathematics and wrote his famous work, 'Elements', which was an exhaustive account of all known mathematics. Although he did not produce many new ideas himself, his ability to rewrite the works of others in an accurate and clear style was such that 'Elements' remains a standard work to the present day.

Two mathematicians inspired by Euclid were Archimedes and Apollonius. The latter's major contribution to mathematics was his work on *conic sections*. When he cut a solid cone in various ways he achieved a series of graceful curves. It was not until later that these conic sections were found to be paths followed by moving bodies under the influence of gravity, such as projectiles, satellites or planets around stars.

The Great Library at Alexandria and a papyrus 'book'.

A parabolic reflector that gives a parallel beam of light, is a practical example of a conic section.

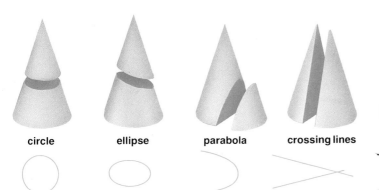

The elliptical orbits of planets.

Conic sections
Cutting parallel to the base gives a circle, but cutting at an angle gives an ellipse. Cutting parallel to one side gives a parabola, cutting through the axis gives crossing lines. Cutting parallel to the axis gives a hyperbola.

circle   ellipse   parabola   crossing lines   hyperbola

Archimedes was the more famous and creative, and is regarded as one of the top three mathematicians, along with Newton and Gauss. He himself was most proud of his proof that the volume of a sphere is equal to two-thirds of the volume of the smallest cylinder that will enclose it. At his request, his diagram of the cylinder and sphere was inscribed on his tombstone when he died in 212 BC. He applied similar techniques to measuring the area of the conic sections.

A sphere enclosed by the smallest possible cylinder. The volume of the sphere is $\frac{2}{3}$ that of the cylinder.

Eureka!

The volume of water overflowing from Archimedes' bathtub was the same as his volume immersed in the water.

Archimedes is well remembered for the story that he ran naked through the streets of his home town Syracuse in Sicily, shouting, 'Eureka, Eureka!' ('I have found it'). While bathing he had discovered a basic law of physics – that an object floating in water displaces its own weight of water, and an object lowered into water appears to lose weight equal to the weight of the water pushed out of the way. At the time he was thinking about a problem he had been set, which was to find out if a crown of gold made for the King of Syracuse had in fact been made partly of silver by an unscrupulous court jeweller. Using his new-found principle, plus some *geometric algebra*, he was able to determine how much silver had been substituted for gold.

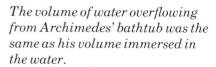

The weight of water flowing into the beaker is equal to the weight of the wooden boat.

Gold is heavier than silver, so the weight of water displaced was less than if the crown had been made of pure gold.

Because the Greeks had no easy way of representing large numbers, Archimedes developed a system for doing so based on the Greek 'myriad' of 10 000. With myriads of myriads multiplied by themselves a myriad myriad of times he reached 'numbers of the first period'. This vast number could then again be multiplied by itself a myriad myriad number of times. This gave, he felt, quite an adequate number! We would have to write it as 1 followed by eighty thousand billion zeros.

Archimedes also discovered the mathematical laws of levers and pulleys, and methods of determining the centre of gravity of an object. He was probably the greatest engineer of ancient times, yet he refused to include his work on engineering in his writings. He thought his reputation as a mathematician would be harmed rather than enhanced by his work as an engineer – the influence of Plato with his contempt for practical applications of mathematics was still strong. He designed engines of war to defend Syracuse from the invading Roman armies. Unfortunately, in 212 BC, after three years of siege, the Romans entered the harbour. Archimedes, at the age of seventy-five, was struck down by a Roman soldier while pondering some geometric problem drawn out in the sand of the courtyard.

His death marked the start of a rapid decline in Greek mathematics, engulfed by the rising Roman Empire.

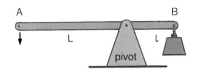

In a lever, a downward force at A at a distance L from the pivot produces an upward force at B. By the principle of levers $B = A \frac{l}{l}$, a small force at A produces a large force at B.

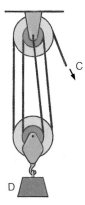

In a pulley, the force needed at C is $\frac{1}{4}$ of the weight D. (1 divided by the number of strings between the pulleys.)

Hipparchus (c. 150 BC) was an astronomer who compiled a list of over one thousand fixed stars. He also made star maps using latitude and longitude. His interest in fixing the positions of stars led him to make a table of sines (the ratios of two of the three sides of right-angled triangles). He used them to calculate that the distance of the moon from the earth was a quarter of a million miles (only five per cent out). His work was the basis for the studies and maps of Ptolemy 300 years later. His last recorded observation was in 126 BC.

The decline of Greek mathematics

A long line of eminent Greek mathematicians finally came to an end. There was no encouragement from the Romans and much of the Greek learning in geometry was left unused. It was not until about AD 300 that Alexandria once again became an important centre of learning. In the interval, however, an interest in *mechanics* and astronomy persisted. Menelaus, living about AD 100, made an important contribution with his work on *spherical trigonometry* (in other words, triangles drawn on the surface of a sphere) and on other properties of ordinary triangles.

Ptolemy (AD 100–168) was a geometer who studied astronomy and map making. His theory that the moon, planets and sun moved around the Earth was adopted by the Arabs and spread into Medieval Europe. This belief was to stand for many centuries until replaced by the theories of Copernicus, who proved that the Earth in fact moves round the sun. Ptolemy collected the work of earlier astronomers in his book 'Almagest'.

The school of Alexandria regained its importance for a time with the work of Hero, Pappus and Diophantus. Hero was not Greek, but probably Egyptian, and very much influenced by Archimedes. He applied his mathematics to engineering and made several new discoveries in geometry and physics. He is even believed to have invented a steam engine. His work also included some optics, and his theorem 'The principle of least action', which states that light travels the shortest possible distance between two points, is fundamental to Einstein's 'Theory of Relativity.'

Pappus worked on many subjects, in particular he was interested in the surface area enclosing the greatest space. Observations of a beehive showed him that bees make hexagonal (six-sided) cells, which require the least amount of wax to enclose the largest area. Triangular or square cells would still pack together but would use more wax.

The third of these mathematicians, Diophantus, was best known for his work on algebra and is often referred to as the 'Father of Algebra'. His particular contribution to algebra was in creating symbols to represent some of the mathematical operations. In this way he was able to write down his thoughts in a systematic and short-hand version. Until this time equations had had to be written out in long-hand and were thus difficult to follow. He also studied *indeterminate equations* (as had Archimedes) where there is no single solution, but a whole family of possible solutions stretching to infinity. By his study of algebra he initiated work into the purest form of pure mathematics, that of 'number theory', where properties of whole numbers such as

Spherical geometry concerns shapes drawn on and within spheres, as distinct from plane geometry where the shapes are drawn on flat surfaces. It is important for global navigation and astronomy.

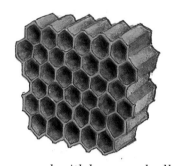

Honeycomb with hexagonal cells.

Diophantus' symbols
He would write 250 x^2 as $\mathbf{\Delta\gamma\sigma\upsilon}$ where $\mathbf{\Delta\gamma}$ meant the square of the unknown x, $\mathbf{\sigma}$ was 200 and $\mathbf{\upsilon}$ was 50. He had no addition sign but used $\pitchfork$ for minus, ι for equals and a special phrase for division.

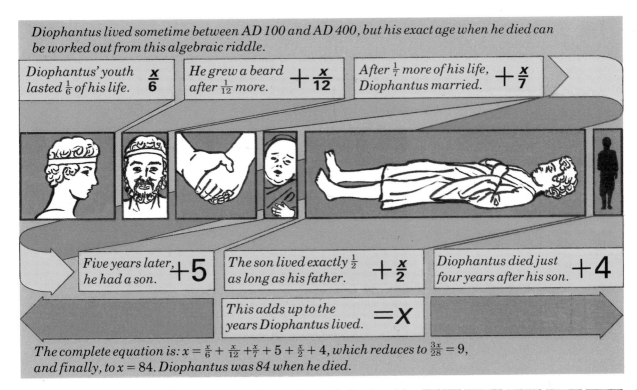

Diophantus lived sometime between AD 100 and AD 400, but his exact age when he died can be worked out from this algebraic riddle.

Diophantus' youth lasted $\frac{1}{6}$ of his life. $\frac{x}{6}$

He grew a beard after $\frac{1}{12}$ more. $+\frac{x}{12}$

After $\frac{1}{7}$ more of his life, Diophantus married. $+\frac{x}{7}$

Five years later, he had a son. $+5$

The son lived exactly $\frac{1}{2}$ as long as his father. $+\frac{x}{2}$

Diophantus died just four years after his son. $+4$

This adds up to the years Diophantus lived. $=X$

The complete equation is: $x = \frac{x}{6} + \frac{x}{12} + \frac{x}{7} + 5 + \frac{x}{2} + 4$, which reduces to $\frac{3x}{28} = 9$, and finally, to $x = 84$. Diophantus was 84 when he died.

odds, evens, *primes* and *squares* are investigated. It should be remembered that the Greeks were still at this time using a very clumsy number system with letters of their alphabet used as numbers. They had no *negative numbers* and no zero.

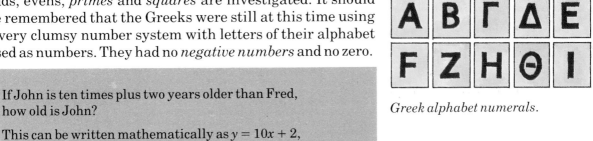

Greek alphabet numerals.

If John is ten times plus two years older than Fred, how old is John?

This can be written mathematically as $y = 10x + 2$, where y is John's age and x is Fred's age.

Here we have one equation, but two unknown quantities x and y.

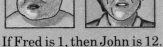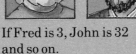

If Fred is 1, then John is 12.

If Fred is 3, John is 32 and so on.

This is an indeterminate equation as we do not have sufficient facts to be able to solve it. If there are as many equations as there are unknown facts, then it becomes a determinate equation.

The last of the pagan mathematicians of Alexandria was the beautiful and very learned woman, Hepatia, who attracted many students to her lectures and edited the works of Diophantus. She died a horrible death at the hands of a Christian mob around AD 400. With her, the remarkable influence of the Greeks on mathematics perished, not to be revived for a thousand years.

The Romans' systematic use of numbers

The Romans brought to an end the great advances of the Greek mathematicians, but we still owe to the Romans many of the words and symbols used in our everyday life. The Roman number system, with which you may be quite familiar, is based on the unit ten, and was less cumbersome than that of the Egyptians. A single stroke I is used to represent 1, repeated up to four times before introducing V to represent 5, X to represent 10 and so on (see diagram). Using the Roman system only fifteen numerals are needed to represent 999 whereas the Egyptians had to use twenty-seven. The Romans at first simply added these numerals to achieve a particular number, for instance, 16 could be written XIV, XVI or IXV. Later they reduced the number of numerals needed by placing them in such a way as to indicate whether a numeral should be added or subtracted from its neighbour. Whereas XVI meant 10 plus 5 plus 1 (sixteen), fourteen was represented by XIV, meaning 10 plus 1 less than 5. Note that 14 now only takes three numerals, not five as before (XIIII). Roman numerals are still to be seen on many public buildings, even modern ones, and on the introductory pages of books and on clock faces. In this latter case, however, 4 is usually seen as IIII rather than IV because it balances the VIII better visually.

From street plans and fort layouts it is evident that the Romans had mastered measurement and land surveying, and used these to impressive effect in their buildings. Many Latin words relating to numbers are still to be found in our language today, the most important being decem (ten), as in decimal. From the list in the table you might like to identify words to do with numbers and measurements derived from the Latin.

I	unus
II	duo
III	tres
IV	quattuor
V	quinque
VI	sex
VII	septem
VIII	octo
IX	novem
X	decem

Plan of Roman fort.

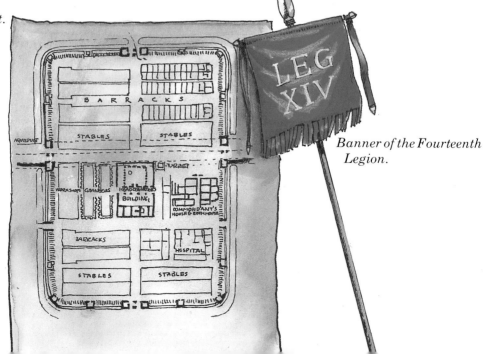

Banner of the Fourteenth Legion.

China

The ancient Chinese civilization was cut off from the rest of the world by high mountains in the west, the sea to the east and dense forests to the south. In the north, invading barbarians were kept at bay by the Great Wall. This was one of the reasons why Chinese mathematics failed to develop beyond the purely practical. However, they did have a decimal system and it is known that Pythagoras was influenced by eastern teaching; it is possible that some of his geometry came from Chinese writings. The Chinese would have used this geometry and some elementary trigonometry to construct their buildings and the Great Wall.

The ancient Chinese were remarkable for their inventiveness – everything from water-powered mills (about 30 BC), the wheelbarrow and the stirrup for use in riding horses (AD 300), to gun powder (AD 900). But the most important inventions to filter through to our civilization were the magnetic compass, paper and printing. The compass became invaluable to the intrepid sea-voyagers of the Renaissance in the 15th century, and paper and printing were vital to the spread of new learning.

'Magic Squares' are also thought to have originated in China around 1000 BC and became a favourite mathematical puzzle all over the world. Two examples are illustrated. The 'magical' property is that rows, columns and diagonals all add up to the same number.

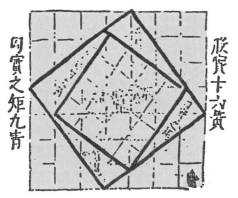

This early Chinese picture suggests that they were familiar with 'Pythagoras' theorem' of right-angled triangles at the time he was alive, and may have discovered it before him.

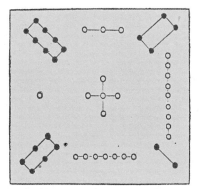

This was the first magic square, constructed about 1000 BC in China. The black dots represent even (female) numbers and the circles odd (male) numbers.

8	3	4
1	5	9
6	7	2

The magic number is 15.

The Venetian explorer, Marco Polo (1254–1324), visited China between 1271 and 1295 and accounts of his travels were widely read in manuscript form – however on his deathbed he said, 'I did not tell half of what I saw; I knew it would not be believed'.

The Chinese failed to fulfil their early promise in mathematics because of their system of writing in pictures which could not express simple things in a simple way. This also meant that knowledge and learning were the privilege of a few scholars, so that the rulers were able to keep the vast majority of the population in ignorance and poverty.

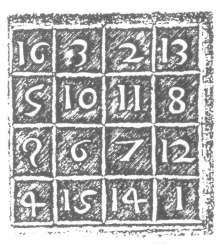

Albrecht Dürer's square. The magic number is 34. The four centre squares also add up to 34. The date it was devised (1514) is included in the bottom row.

The Islamic influence

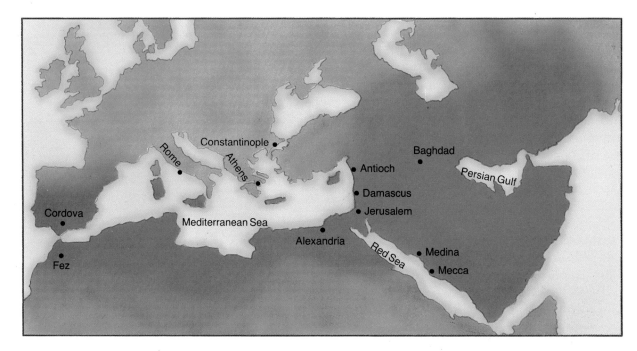

Islam is the name given to the huge empire rapidly acquired by the Moslems, the followers of Mohammed. Born a poor shepherd boy in Mecca (in Arabia), Mohammed rejected the Arabian belief in many gods in favour of a belief in a single god that he called Allah. From the year 622, which became year one of the new Islamic calendar, he was to initiate an incredible expansion of the Islamic Empire, stretching from Spain and Southern France in the west, to the borders of India in the east. What was so remarkable about this rapid expansion was the way in which the Moslems absorbed so much of the culture of the people they conquered. Unfortunately much of the Greek work was destroyed (as at Alexandria), but a great deal of it was still available and was studied and translated into Arabic. Trade with the Hindus in India added to this store of knowledge, the most significant result of which was the adoption of their decimal system. Baghdad had become the new centre of learning.

It is not clear how much contact there had been in earlier times between the Greek scholars and the Hindus, although Alexander the Great had reached as far as India. Certainly the Hindus had a number system based on ten which was similar to that rf the Egyptians. This was modified by an unknown Hindu mathematician. He realized that symbols for numbers greater than nine were unnecessary. Careful positioning of the nine symbols could represent a number of ones, a number of tens, or hundreds and so on. At first, a space was left between columns if, say, there were no tens,

The extent of the Islamic Empire in the 10th century (shown in red).

only ones and hundreds (for example, two hundred and three), but it was difficult to tell if a gap represented one empty column or two. Another Hindu had the idea of using a symbol '0' for nothing. With this improvement there now existed the best number system ever invented, much simpler to use in arithmetic than any other. Try doing a long division using Roman numerals!

Because of the Moslems' readiness to absorb new ideas, and because of the size of their empire, this new system spread rapidly over Northern Africa and into Spain. In the rest of Western Europe, however, learning was at a low ebb in the period called the Dark Ages, and Arabic numerals were slow to be accepted. A Frenchman, Gerbert, travelled to Spain in AD 967 where he studied the Arabic numerals. He came across the book of Muhammed Al-Khwarizmi, an Arabian mathematician, who was the first to write about the use of the Hindu system in arithmetic. Gerbert took this new knowledge back to France but even when he became Pope Sylvester II he found it almost impossible to persuade Europeans to use the Hindu system.

The title of Al-Khwarizmi's book was 'al-jabr w'al-muqabalah', which means 'the art of bringing together unknowns to match a known quantity'. Our word 'algebra' (meaning 'bringing together') comes from this title. The Hindu, Mahavira (AD 850) gave the rules we use today for dividing and multiplying fractions. Progress was also made in spherical trigonometry and map making, stimulated by long trading voyages to Africa and the East.

The Moslem scholars improved upon the astronomical tables of the Alexandrians and Hindus. They also became aware of the possibility of negative numbers and realized that there was both a positive and negative solution to an equation like $x^2 = 4$; $x = 2$ and $x = -2$, since $2 \times 2 = 4$ and $-2 \times -2 = 4$. It was many years later, when Western Europe emerged from the Dark Ages, however, before this proposition was really taken seriously.

Confusion before the zero was introduced.

2 3

Did this mean two hundred and three or two thousand and three? It depended on how large you made the gap.

203

Placing a zero in the tens column leaves us in no doubt.

Long division with Roman numerals.

A fights B   *B fights C*   *So A and C are friends.*

$-2 \times -2 = 4$

A minus times a minus makes a plus, or an enemy's enemy is a friend!

19

The revival of mathematics in Europe

The Dark Ages in Europe came as a result of the decline and fall of the Roman Empire as it was overrun by Germanic tribes. Such reading and writing as survived was mostly confined to keeping the Christian doctrine alive. The Church, in particular the monks, dominated all; to them the most important calculations were the fixing of Easter and working out the tithes, or rents, due to them. However, the Head of the Holy Roman Empire, Charlemagne, was more liberal and invited Alcuin (735–804), an English church leader from York, to supervise his court school. Alcuin encouraged the study of Greece and Rome, and set up a schedule of learning, later called the Seven Liberal Arts. These included arithmetic, geometry and astronomy. He also devised problems 'for the quickening of the mind'; for an example, see the picture below.

All books had to be copied by hand until the invention of printing.

This sparked off a series of revivals of interest in learning, leading eventually to the Renaissance (literally: rebirth) of the 15th century, centred in Northern Italy. An upturn in trade led to the need for more calculating in business. The Italian merchants soon discovered the value of the Arabic numerals and rapidly abandoned the more clumsy Roman ones. However, they ceased to use the Arabic word for nothing, 'sifr', substituting their own word 'zepiro', from which we get our 'zero'.

The first new advance in mathematics was made by Scipione del Ferro (1465–1526), a paper-maker's son, who

Wolves eat goats and goats eat cabbages. A ferryman has a wolf, a goat and a cabbage, but he can only take one across the river at a time. How did he get all three across uneaten?

had risen to become Professor of Mathematics at the University of Bologna. He found a solution to the *cubic equation* (for example, $x^3 + mx = n$), a problem which had always baffled the Greeks. However, he kept this find to himself for some thirty years before he was forced to disclose it in one of the many intellectual disputes of that time.

Leonardo da Pisa (1170–1250) had tackled the problem of negative numbers while working on his accounts. "This problem", he concluded, "I have shown to be insoluble unless it is conceded that the first man had a debt". This idea of giving away more than you actually have is one way of thinking of negative numbers in practical terms. However, this mathematical idea was not to be fully accepted until 1545, when Cardano, in his work on equations 'Ars Magna' (Great Art), set out the laws that govern them. His other very significant contribution was the idea of the *square root* of a negative number, which he called 'fictitious' or 'sophistic'. Since no *real number*, multiplied by itself, can produce a negative number, the square root of a negative number is now called an *imaginary number*. An imaginary number combined with a real number forms a *complex number*. This concept has proved to be of immense value to later mathematicians, scientists and engineers, and is fundamental to some of the work of the great mathematician Gauss in the 19th century (see page 34).

With these early Italian mathematicians a breakthrough into new knowledge far beyond that of the Greek scholars had begun. The introduction of paper and printing was to speed this new era on its way.

A student of Scipione, **Antonio Fior**, took on another notable mathematician, Nicolo Fontana, nick-named **Tortaglia** because of his stammer, in a 'duel' in solving cubic equations. Tortaglia won easily, but came up against stiffer opposition in **Girolamo Cardano**, the illegitimate son of a lawyer. Cardano was not what one might expect in an eminent mathematician: he was a compulsive gambler, frequently in debt and risked being burnt at the stake for disagreeing with the Church's teaching. Such was his good luck, however, that the Pope himself gave him a pension and Tortaglia gave him his general solution for cubic equations. This he later published, much to the annoyance of Tortaglia.

The merchants in this busy Italian port found Arabic numbers much easier to use in their calculations than Roman ones.

Theory and practice are re-united

With the spread of learning over Europe, a new stimulus to mathematics in solving practical problems was provided. People wanted to explore more of the world but, because of the Turkish invasion of Constantinople in 1453, overland trade routes to the East were blocked. Navigation and charting of unknown coastlines along newly discovered sea routes became vital. Sailors could estimate their position of latitude from the angle of the Polar Star using an astrolabe, but finding their precise longitude was more difficult and needed an accurate chronometer – or clock suitable for use at sea. Until one was devised in about 1750 by an Englishman, John Harrison, either ships kept close to land, or else estimated distances travelled from a rough measurement of their speed.

In the field of astronomy there was a rising conflict between scientists and the Church. Copernicus, born in 1473 in Poland, rejected the Ptolemaic idea of the Earth as the focus of the universe, believing instead that the sun was at the centre. He did not publish his work until just before his death and even then it was regarded as a mathematical exercise rather than an astronomical treatise; it was almost a century before it was condemned by the Church.

Tycho Brahe (1546–1601), a Danish astronomer, disagreed with the Copernican school of thought and set out to restore the Ptolemaic theory. To do so he made amazingly accurate records of 777 stars, using a refined version of the astrolabe. Shortly before he died he appointed Kepler (1571–1630) as his assistant. Kepler made observations on a further 288 stars and their results showed that the planets did indeed rotate about the sun. In addition Kepler showed that the planets' orbits were elliptical, not circular, as had been thought since Plato's time. He proposed three revolutionary laws of planetary motion and formulated the idea of the sun exerting a 'magnetic' force on the planets, later shown by Newton to be the force of gravity.

An ornate astrolabe. With such an instrument Tycho Brahe made observations accurate to $\frac{1}{60}$ of a degree.

Kepler's 3 laws
1. *The orbit of each planet is an ellipse, with the sun at one focus.*
2. *A line joining the planet to the sun sweeps out equal areas in equal times.*
3. *The square of the period of rotation of the planet is proportional to the cube of its mean distance from the sun.*
   The period of the Earth's rotation is, of course, one year. From his third law, a planet situated twice as far from the sun would take nearly three years to perform its orbit.

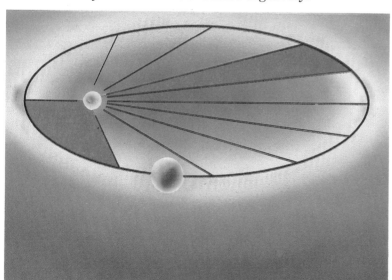

A contemporary of Kepler was Galileo Galilei (1564–1642), born in Pisa, the son of a nobleman. With Galileo we see the real beginnings of modern physical science. In his studies of motion (*dynamics*), he showed the importance of collecting experimental evidence before proposing new theories. He also developed mathematical equations to calculate and describe motion. Galileo is alleged to have dropped pebbles of different sizes from the top of the Leaning Tower of Pisa, to study the effects of gravity on them. He also recognised the constant swing of a pendulum, later to be used in clocks, from watching the swinging of a lamp in the Cathedral of Pisa. Galileo perfected the refracting telescope, which led to his discovery of Jupiter's four major satellites, the rings of Saturn, sun spots and craters on the moon. Like Kepler, he believed in the Copernican view, and although initially allowed to continue his work purely as a mathematical hypothesis, or idea, he was later forced to renounce his theories and publicly declare the superiority of the Church's Ptolemaic views.

The Leaning Tower of Pisa. From his experiments, Galileo found that falling objects of different weights take the same amount of time to reach the ground.

The great artist and inventor Leonardo da Vinci was born at Vinci, near Florence, in 1452. Although not strictly a mathematician, he applied the new geometric technique of perspective to give depth to his pictures and studied perfect proportions in his subjects. He was a great believer in the principle, subsequently followed by Galileo, that observation comes first, followed by careful reasoning to explain these observations.

Leonardo's use of perspective in a design for a new stable.

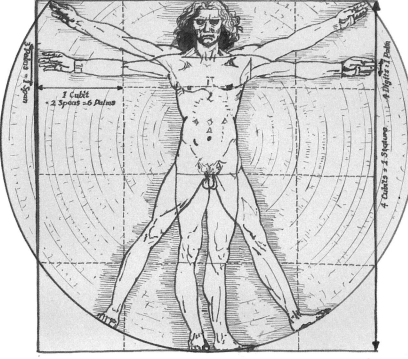

Leonardo's drawing showing the proportions of a human figure in a circle.

Early computing machines

The earliest of all aids to addition must surely be the fingers, and even the toes. To cope with larger numbers, pebbles and sticks were used and then sand or dust tables where lines could be drawn with a piece of stick. The next development was the early abacus, consisting of lines drawn on a table, onto which discs or small objects were placed to indicate numbers. From this, the abacus with which we are more familiar, was derived around 3000 BC in Babylon. Similar to a baby's counting frame, it consists of a frame with wires at regular intervals, and a bar. On the Japanese version there are four beads on one side of the bar. Moving a bead towards the bar represents a count of one. On the other side of the bar there is one bead. Moving one of these beads represents a count of five (see diagram). A skilled operator, such as are still to be found in the Orient, can use an abacus to calculate at amazing speeds.

The Roman version of the abacus often had an extra two wires, one with four and one with twelve beads, to help them with quarters and twelfths. Another variation was designed by Gerbert, the Frenchman who visited Spain in AD 967 and studied the Arabic numerals. His version had beads with the numbers written on them. However, although fewer beads had to be moved, it took longer to use, as it took time to select the correct beads.

The 'line abacus' became widespread across Europe once the Arabic number system had been adopted. No more than four counters ought to be present on any one line and no more than one between each line; when there were five on a line one would be carried across to the next space. From this we get our present idea of 'carrying one', when adding.

Many other simple devices were used for easy reckoning, but the next important development came with 'Napier's Bones', invented by the Scottish mathematician, John Napier (1550–1617). The diagram shows how the rods would

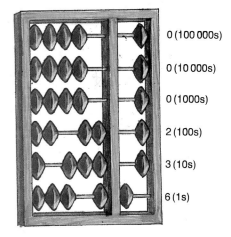

0 (100 000s)
0 (10 000s)
0 (1000s)
2 (100s)
3 (10s)
6 (1s)

This version of an abacus stores the number 236.

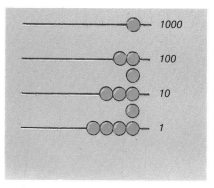

1000
100
10
1

A line abacus showing the number 1289.

Napier's 'Bones'.

To multiply 32 × 8 the appropriate bones are placed together to make up the number 32. Looking at row 8, the answer comes by adding up the numbers on the diagonals.

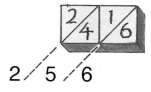

2 5 6

be used to multiply 32 by 8. Like the abacus, the use of the bones became widespread, not only in Europe, but as far afield as China and Japan.

Napier developed the concept of *logarithms*, which are set out in tables and provide a way of using addition and subtraction to perform multiplication and division. Until quite recently books of 'log' tables, with numbers given to four decimal places, were standard issue to pupils in school. Now they have largely been replaced by inexpensive electronic calculators. So too has the slide rule, an ingenious device based on logarithms. Here the addition of the logarithm of the numbers is achieved by adding two lengths together using the moveable centre section. It was designed by Robert Bissaker in 1654, based on work by Edmund Gunter, and William Oughtred.

The numbers on a slide rule are not evenly spaced, but set out as logarithmic scales. To multiply 2 by 3, 1 on the slide (scale C) is placed on the first number to be multiplied on scale D. The cursor is placed on the second number on the slide. The answer is read off on scale D.

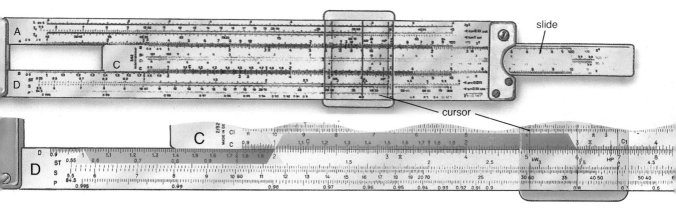

logarithmic length of **2** + logarithmic length of **3** → logarithmic length of **6**

Slightly earlier, in 1642, the nineteen-year-old French mathematician Blaise Pascal (see page 29) devised a mechanical adding machine when he got fed up with adding up on his fingers for his tax-collector father. It had a series of gear wheels and pegs which performed the 'carry' operation, and dials to show the result (see cover picture). Leibnitz improved on Pascal's machine, designing one capable of multiplication and division; but these machines were never a match for the sheer simplicity of the slide rule.

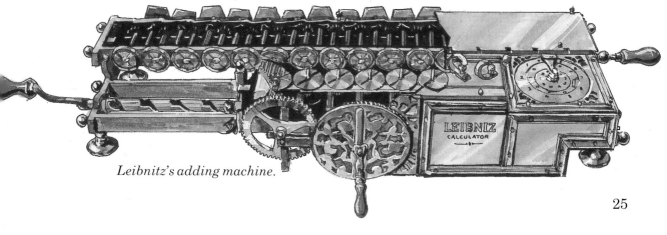

Leibnitz's adding machine.

The great 17th century mathematicians

Towards the end of the 16th century the advancement of mathematics shifted from Northern Italy to France; with such eminent mathematicians as Descartes, Fermat and Pascal.

Trigonometry – the study of triangles – had been used since the days of early Babylon, but mostly as a tool in surveying, astronomy and navigation. The Greeks had tabulated the ratios between any two sides of a right-angled triangle – referred to as the *sine* (or sin), *cosine* (or cos) and *tangent* (or tan). However, Francois Viète noticed that these ratios could be used in the solution of *quadratic equations* – a fact which was to form part of Descartes' work later. Francois Viète, born in 1540, was actually a lawyer working for the King of France and mathematics to him was just a hobby, but one at which he worked extensively. In algebra, he used letters to represent the coefficients of the *variables*, for example, $ax^2 + bx = c$. In this example, the coefficients of x are the letters a and b, and x is a variable. The letter c represents a constant number – one that does not change. By using letters instead of particular numbers it was now possible to prove that the solution to the equation was a general solution for any values of a, b and c.

René Descartes (1596–1650) was born in France, the son of an aristocrat, and graduated in law at the University of Poitiers. However, he was deeply dissatisfied with the classical philosophy that he had been taught and, at the age of twenty, set out to formulate a new philosophy through mathematics. In seeking out the basic truths on which to build his new ideals, he concluded that there was only one – 'I think, therefore I am'. Descartes is regarded as the pioneer of modern philosophy. In mathematics he was to revolutionize the whole approach, bringing all branches together with his *analytical geometry* – the combination of geometry and algebra into the graphs that we know today.

The new idea in analytical geometry was that a position on a surface could be fixed by a pair of numbers called *co-ordinates*. Also all quantities have a direction assigned to them. When moving from one point on the graph to another, it may be in a positive or negative direction. He realized that

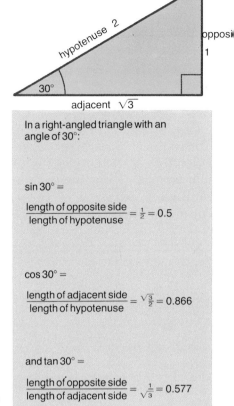

In a right-angled triangle with an angle of 30°:

$\sin 30° =$

$$\frac{\text{length of opposite side}}{\text{length of hypotenuse}} = \tfrac{1}{2} = 0.5$$

$\cos 30° =$

$$\frac{\text{length of adjacent side}}{\text{length of hypotenuse}} = \tfrac{\sqrt{3}}{2} = 0.866$$

and $\tan 30° =$

$$\frac{\text{length of opposite side}}{\text{length of adjacent side}} = \tfrac{1}{\sqrt{3}} = 0.577$$

Moving from Home to Shop 1 is positive.
Moving from Home to Shop 2 is negative.
From Shop 2 to Home is a positive move.
From Shop 1 to Home is a negative move.

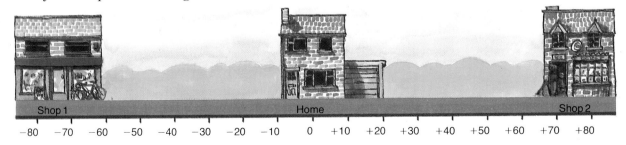

How points are defined on a graph.

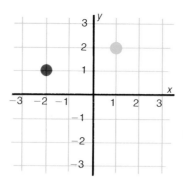

The blue point shown has 'co-ordinates' (1,2) – the distances along the x axis and the y axis respectively.
The red point has co-ordinates (−2,1).

any equation could be represented by a curve on a graph and that any curve (or straight line) could be represented by an equation; although the more complex the curve the longer and more complicated the equation would have to be.

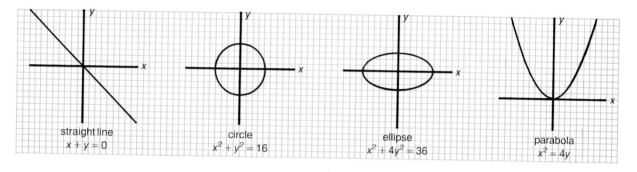

straight line
$x + y = 0$

circle
$x^2 + y^2 = 16$

ellipse
$x^2 + 4y^2 = 36$

parabola
$x^2 = 4y$

Graphs – often called Cartesian graphs after Descartes – provide an important method for determining the nature and number of possible solutions of equations. As well as being applied to geometry, they could also be used in trigonometry. Viète's trigonometric equations, such as $y = \sin x$ could be plotted, which in this case gives the familiar sinusoidal curve. The shape of this curve is now known to occur frequently in nature – as waves in water, alternating current, vibrating strings, and as electromagnetic waves such as light and radio waves.

Curves with their equations.

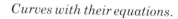

Cathode-ray oscilloscope showing sinusoidal waveform.

Descartes was slow to publish his philosophy and findings, possibly because he was unwilling to suffer the same fate as Galileo, but finally his monumental work 'Discours de la méthode' was published in Holland in 1637. He had taken refuge there, constantly moving from house to house in an attempt to escape from his admirers who plagued him. He was never in very good health and seldom rose from his bed before 11 o'clock in the morning, preferring to do his thinking there in peace.

His death was ironic. The nineteen-year-old Queen of Sweden was so determined to have him as her tutor, that after several unsuccessful attempts to persuade him to come, eventually she sent a battleship to collect him. Against his better judgement he went, but her rigorous life style, starting work at 6 am in a poorly-heated library, was too much for him. After only eleven weeks he contracted influenza and died at the age of fifty-four.

Pierre de Fermat (1601–1665), a leading investigator of number theory, was a Member of Parliament and did not seriously begin to study mathematics until he was thirty – his way of relaxing in his spare time! He wrote several theorems, which were often scrawled in the margin of his copy of Diophantus' 'Arithmetica' as and when they occurred to him. One of his most notable, often called 'Fermat's Last Theorem' (for reasons not too clear, since he went on to write several more) remains unsolved – tantalizingly he wrote 'I have found for this a truly wonderful proof, but the margin is too small to hold it'. He too worked on analytical geometry quite independently of Descartes, but published his findings at a slightly later date, so he did not get much credit for it. However, he took the work further by applying it to solid geometry and conic curves. His application of the idea of infinitesimals – that is, taking minute variations or changes in quantities – was to lead directly onto Newton's work on calculus.

In a completely different area and working with Pascal, Fermat developed the *Theory of Probability*. This arose from a problem he had been asked to solve – how should the 'pot' (money at stake) be divided between the players in an interrupted game of dice? Their conclusion was that the money should be divided according to the chance each player had of winning. This 'Theory of Probability' has had an immense number of applications; from working out life insurance premiums and designing safety systems for power stations, to spot-checking on production lines. Even the behaviour of sub-atomic particles, the building blocks of the universe, can be described in terms of probabilities.

Blaise Pascal was something of an infant prodigy. Born in 1623, he was not at first allowed to study mathematics, but

René Descartes.

$$x^n + y^n = z^n$$

No whole numbers exist for x, y and z to satisfy this equation when n is an integer greater than two.
I have found for this a truly wonderful proof but the margin is too small to hold it.

Fermat's 'Last Theorem'.

28

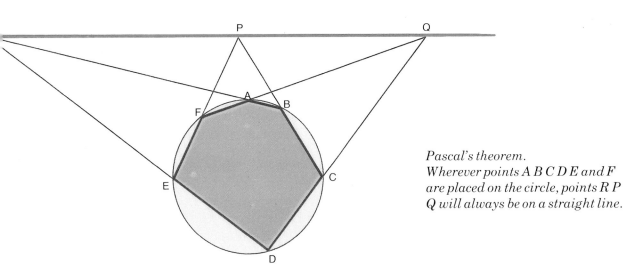

Pascal's theorem.
Wherever points A B C D E and F are placed on the circle, points R P Q will always be on a straight line.

on his own he discovered several of the properties of triangles and other figures. When found out, his father relented and he was given a copy of Euclid's 'Elements' to study, which he quickly mastered. At the age of sixteen he wrote an essay on conics (shapes formed by cutting up cones), which Descartes at first refused to accept as having been written by Pascal. At nineteen he built his calculating machine (see page 25).

He was interested in *projective geometry* and proved the theorem illustrated in the diagram, and from this proof went on to work out over four hundred propositions which naturally followed on. He was deeply religious and twice gave up mathematics to study his beliefs. As well as his theorem, he also gave his name to a triangle used for calculating probabilities. Besides his study of mathematics he carried out important experiments in hydrostatics, the study of fluids.

His health was never very good and his continual study drove him to an early death at the age of only thirty-nine.

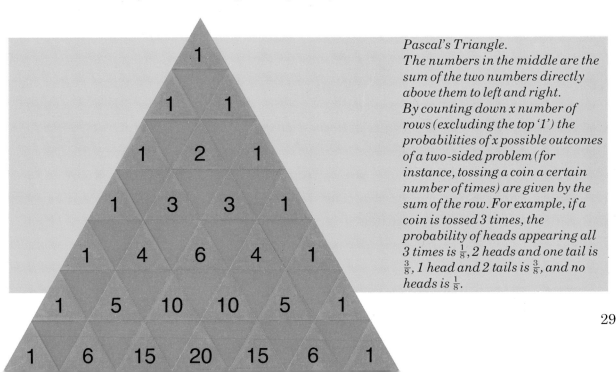

Pascal's Triangle.
The numbers in the middle are the sum of the two numbers directly above them to left and right. By counting down x number of rows (excluding the top '1') the probabilities of x possible outcomes of a two-sided problem (for instance, tossing a coin a certain number of times) are given by the sum of the row. For example, if a coin is tossed 3 times, the probability of heads appearing all 3 times is $\frac{1}{8}$, 2 heads and one tail is $\frac{3}{8}$, 1 head and 2 tails is $\frac{3}{8}$, and no heads is $\frac{1}{8}$.

Sir Isaac Newton

When we think of gravity, we often think of Sir Isaac Newton, sitting under an apple tree. Newton was one of the giants of modern science and the author of the 'Principia Mathematica' (1687), recognized as one of the most influential, conclusive and revolutionary works ever to appear in print. He typifies our idea of the absent-minded professor: it is reported that once, while he was entertaining guests to dinner, he left the room to get a bottle of wine, only to be found some time later in his study, engrossed in some new problem, quite forgetting he had guests at all.

On graduating from Cambridge, he began work on his theory of universal gravitation, movement of the planets and his version of calculus. He returned to lecture at Cambridge in 1667 in numerous subjects, including optics, the study of light. His paper on the theory that white light was made up of all the colours of the rainbow, caused great astonishment to the Royal Society. His professor at Cambridge, Sir Isaac Barrow, had realized that the problem of tangents and areas under curves were two sides of the same coin, but it was Newton who developed the ideas of his eminent predecessors into calculus. Barrow generally admitted that Newton had achieved what he himself had failed to do, and on his retirement was instrumental in having Newton appointed as his successor to the chair of mathematics at the incredibly young age of twenty-six.

Over the next forty years, Newton made many important contributions to science. Albert Einstein said of him, "Nature to him was an open book, whose letters he could read without effort." But Newton was a modest man who said of himself, "I do not know what I may appear to the world, but to myself I seem to have been merely a boy playing on the seashore, diverting myself in now and then finding a smoother pebble or a prettier shell than others, whilst the great ocean of Truth lay all undiscovered before me."

Newton was always slow to publish his results; whether it was because of his reluctance to deal with the arguments

Sir Isaac Newton was born in Lincolnshire on Christmas Day, 1642. He received a basic education at the local schools and when only 12 was sent away to King's School, Grantham. At 19 he went to Trinity College, Cambridge, and graduated without special distinction. In 1666, while studying for his Master's degree, the College was closed because of the Great Plague so he returned home to Lincolnshire. There he really developed his ideas about gravitation and optics, and as a result, when he returned to Cambridge in 1667 he quickly finished his Master's degree. He stayed in Cambridge for a further 27 years and, with the publication of his 'Principia', lost interest in scientific matters and turned instead to University politics. Elected to represent the University in Parliament in 1696, he was appointed Master of the Mint. He received the first knighthood given for scientific achievement, and was elected life president of the Royal Society. He died in 1727 at the age of 85.

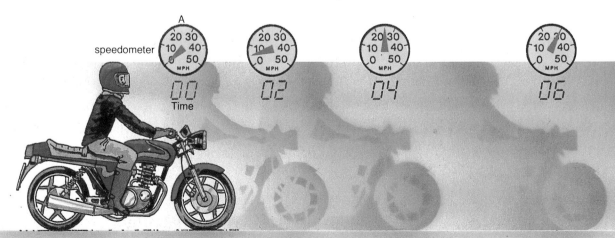

speedometer

which met each of his new discoveries, or because he was always too busy with new ideas to take time off to write up the previous ones, it is hard to know. Certainly he was not much of a talker: his only known utterance as a Member of Parliament was when he asked if a window might be opened. Unfortunately, this slowness led him into a bitter dispute with Leibnitz, a German mathematician. Leibnitz invented his own version of calculus 10 years after Newton, but he published his findings first.

The importance of calculus is that it allows a mathematical description of the process of change. Virtually everything in the universe is changing. People grow older, and things are constantly in motion or changing position. But the process of change is difficult to analyse. Because it is continuous it is hard to track down. It baffled mathematicians until the invention of calculus.

Using calculus, Newton was able to deduce his three laws of motion and his crowning achievement, the 'Law of Universal Gravitation'. This law describes the behaviour of all moving bodies. Calculus has become the principle link between practical science and engineering and pure mathematical thought.

At the age of eighty-five, Newton died and received the final honour of being buried in Westminster Abbey. Throughout his life he had always acknowledged the work of the mathematicians who had prepared the ground before him: "If I have seen further than other men, it is because I have stood on the shoulders of giants."

Calculus analyses motion by measuring rates of change. This may be represented by tangents to a curve on a Cartesian graph. The total amount of change is represented by the area under the curve. The process for finding the tangent or gradient of a curve at any point is called differentiation and for the area under a curve, integration.

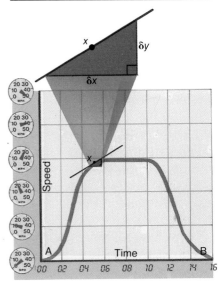

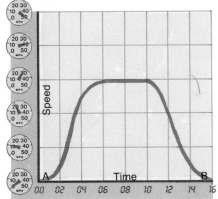

A motorcyclist starts from the traffic lights, and accelerates to a maximum speed of 30 miles per hour, then slows down and stops at the next traffic lights.
The graph shows how his speed changes with time. The slope of the graph at any time shows his acceleration and the area under the graph his total distance covered.

At point x on the graph the slope of the tangent is given by $\delta y/\delta x$. The area is found by adding together all the strips of width δx.

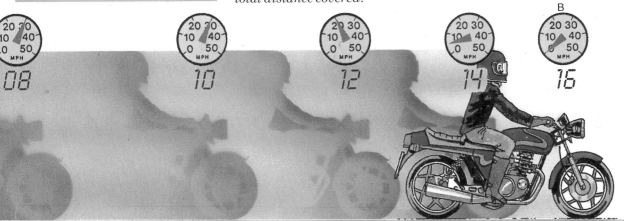

18th century mathematics

Much of 18th century mathematics was concerned with the application and development of the new calculus and analytical geometry. The great rivalry which had arisen between Newton and Leibnitz was carried on by their successors. The remarkable Swiss Bernoulli family, with no fewer than eight leading mathematicians in three generations, were supporters of Leibnitz. They did much to spread calculus throughout Europe. The advantage of Leibnitz's method was his superior *notation*. He used the expression dy/dx to represent the fractional change in measurement y corresponding to the fractional change in measurement x, which is at the heart of calculus. Newton wrote this fractional change, or *differential*, of y as y (dot notation).

One of the triumphs of calculus was the description of planetary motion. Observations had shown that the planets did not move in perfectly elliptical orbits as required by Kepler's laws. Instead, irregularities were found. Using calculus and Newton's Law of Universal Gravitation it was shown that these were caused by the gravitational forces of the planets on each other, acting in addition to the gravitational force of the sun.

Despite its uses, the methods of calculus were strongly attacked by Bishop Berkeley, an Irish philosopher. He declared that instantaneous rates of change were "neither finite quantities, nor quantities infinitely small, nor yet nothing" but were the "ghosts of departed quantities!"

Perhaps the most able mathematician of the time was Leonhard Euler. He introduced a number of useful notations and theorems. He studied magic squares and *topology* and did practical work on ship building and gunnery. He also developed and extended the use of calculus. An Italian, Joseph Lagrange (1736–1813), also worked extensively with calculus, but neither he nor Euler were able to bring order to the subject. This was achieved in 1821 by the French mathematician Augustin-Louis Cauchy.

Using the tool of calculus, scientists continued their search for the mathematical laws of nature.

Leonhard Euler (1707–1783) (his name is pronounced 'oiler') was born in Basel, Switzerland. When only 20 he was invited by the Empress, Catherine I of Russia, to join the Academy of Science at St Petersburg. After 3 years he was made Professor of Physics and later Professor of Mathematics. In 1741 he moved to Berlin to become Director of Mathematics at the Academy of Science, but returned to St Petersburg in 1766 as Director of the Academy. Sadly, he soon became blind, but this did not stop his work and he dictated many more books and papers. During his distinguished academic career he made numerous contributions in all fields of mathematics.

Euler's formula.
Euler showed that in any many-sided figure, or polyhedron, the number of edges plus 2 is always equal to the number of vertices (corners) plus the number of sides. Thus, a cube has 8 vertices and 6 sides, and therefore 12 edges. The stellated octahedron (made up of 8 tetrahedrons) has 8 vertices, 24 sides and 30 edges. The formula $e + 2 = v + s$ works for any polyhedron.

cube or hexahedron　　　　**stellated octahedron**

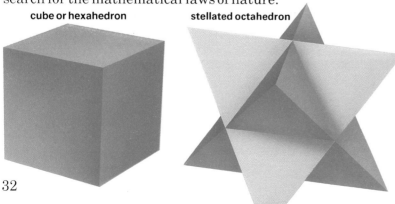

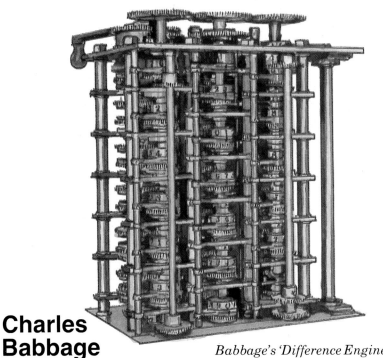

Charles Babbage

Babbage's 'Difference Engine'.

Charles Babbage is best known for his designs for early mechanical computers, but he also played a small but important part in the dispute between Newton and Leibnitz. Together with some friends he formed a society to promote the superior Continental ideas in England, and in particular to banish the 'dottage' of Cambridge, a reference to the dot notation of Newton.

Babbage was to be recognized as a man far ahead of his time. His first machine, called a 'Difference Engine', was designed to calculate and print out mathematical tables, but after spending £17 000 (a vast sum in those days) including a government grant of £1000, he gave it up, as he could not get the parts made sufficiently accurately for it to work. Undeterred, he went on to design an even grander machine which he called an 'Analytical Machine' – to be driven by steam. This design incorporated all the basic elements of a modern computer. It was to be programmable and capable of performing all types of calculation, to contain a memory or store and a central processing unit (which he called the mill), and to have an input unit using punched cards and a paper printing output. However, this machine was never built through lack of funds. We know so much about it from the writings of Ada Augusta, the Countess of Lovelace, who was herself a mathematician (and the daughter of Lord Byron). She realized the importance of what Babbage was attempting and wrote detailed notes on his design. Sadly for Babbage, working versions of the 'Difference Engine' were built in Sweden, and the British Government bought one to work out life expectancy tables for the Registrar General's Office.

Lady Lovelace.

Karl Friedrich Gauss

The German genius Karl Friedrich Gauss dominated the mathematics of the 19th century. As a child he was brilliant and is said to have found a mistake in his father's accounts at the age of three. He studied the classics in addition to geometry, algebra and calculus. At the age of 19 he proved that a regular polygon with a prime number of sides (17) could be constructed with a pair of compasses and a ruler, something thought impossible by the Greeks. He was so delighted that he decided to devote his life to mathematics and the sciences.

He first achieved fame in astronomy. In 1801, the minor planet, or asteroid, named Ceres was discovered. However, after a few measurements of its motion and position, it disappeared from view in the bright region of sky near the sun. Astronomers throughout Europe were excited by this discovery and they tried to calculate exactly where Ceres would reappear in the sky. Gauss was the first to calculate a theoretical orbit for Ceres and astronomers found it where Gauss predicted it would be. Gauss was honoured by learned societies everywhere for this achievement and became the leading figure of European mathematics for the next 50 years.

One of Gauss's greatest contributions to mathematics was in theoretical algebra and its practical applications. Descartes had invented the system of representing positions by co-ordinates on a graph. On Cartesian graphs, lines had direction as well as length. Gauss realized that such lines, or *vectors* could be used to represent forces, *velocities* and *accelerations*. He then showed how these vectors could be represented graphically in a new way using 'complex numbers'. Complex numbers are difficult to understand; they are numbers composed of a 'real' number and an 'imaginary' number. An example of a complex number is $2 + 4\sqrt{-1}$ where 2 is the real part and $4\sqrt{-1}$, usually written as $4i$, is the imaginary part. The important point about complex numbers is that they behave mathematically in the same way as vectors. Mathematicians find it easy to

Karl Friedrich Gauss, born in 1777 the son of a German bricklayer, was, like Mozart and Pascal, an infant prodigy. He was a brilliant scholar in the classics and languages but was at first undecided whether to pursue mathematics or philosophy. Throughout his career he travelled little and, like Newton, was reluctant to have his work published. The vast scope of the work that he had done became apparent after his death in 1855, when his copious notes were published.

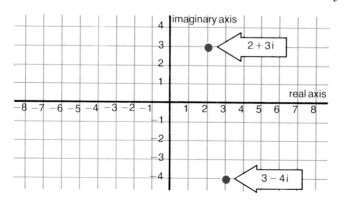

Complex numbers shown on a Cartesian graph.

Computer graphic design involves ➤ *mapping complex curved surfaces which can then be viewed from any direction.*

34

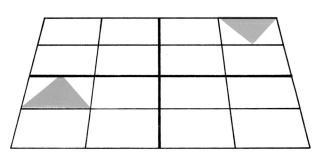

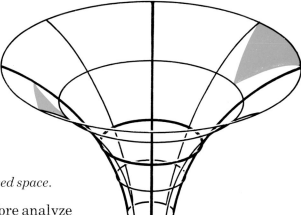

Flat and curved space.

do algebra with complex numbers and can therefore analyze very complicated problems with many forces, or vectors, acting at once.

Gauss went even further in his use of complex numbers, incorporating them into a special type of calculus used in solving many types of scientific and engineering problems – differential equations. These represent one of the highest forms of mathematical creativity and are an important part of modern mathematical thought on the structure of the universe.

Gauss's studies even led him to question the nature of space itself. If lines and surfaces could be curved, then why not space? This seemingly impossible idea was followed up by a number of people including a pupil of Gauss, Bernhard Riemann. He was asked by Gauss to give a lecture on the subject and obliged by describing an entirely new geometry of space without using a single diagram or equation. Gauss was probably the only other person to understand it!

As one new concept leads on to another, so these revolutionary ideas were to be taken up and brought to a climax fifty years later by the physicist Albert Einstein, in his theories of relativity.

Like Newton, Gauss was reluctant to publish his work. For every idea he produced in public, many more thoughts and studies lay untouched in his papers to be discovered after his death. He influenced many branches of science and his work with the physicist Wilhelm Weber on electricity and *magnetism* is marked by the use of their names as units of magnetism. They also devised a workable telegraph system of communication 2 years before Samuel B. Morse.

Albert Einstein (1879–1955) was born in Germany. He did not show much early promise, although clearly he had an enquiring mind. At 15 he was deeply influenced by Euclid's writings and went on rapidly to master integral and differential calculus. His first job after gaining his diploma from the Federal Institute of Technology in Zurich, was at the Patents Office in Bern. While there he wrote the first of his revolutionary scientific papers. These papers brought him fame and he was much sought after by universities in Europe. However, there was anti-Jewish feeling in Germany, and so he moved to California in 1933. Six years later he played a key role in the research that led to the first atomic bomb. When it was finally used to destroy Hiroshima in 1945 Einstein, a pacifist and humanitarian, was deeply distressed. He died in America in 1955.

From calculating machine to computer

Throughout this book it has been seen that new advances are not usually made by just one person. People credited with an invention bring together the work of several other people in a new way, and are led to do so by the needs of the society in which they live. This is shown by the history of the computer over the last one hundred years. How the lives of ordinary people changed over the centuries has been well described in other books in this series, and it is these changes that produced the need for rapid and accurate computation. While Babbage was building his 'Difference Engine' – at the same time as James Watt was building his steam engine – the urgent need for this type of calculation had not arisen. That need was to come much later.

Rapid *data* handling by machine was first tried for the 1890 population census of America, because the results for the previous census in 1880 had taken so long to work out. The machine, designed by an American statistician, Herman Hollerith, used punched cards to feed in the information. This type of card was not a new idea, but had been invented by Joseph Jacquard in 1801 for a silk weaving loom. An endless belt of punched cards controlled the pattern making process by having needles which either slipped through a hole in the card or were blocked by it. With Hollerith's machine it took only six weeks to work out that the total population was over sixty-two million. So successful was it that Hollerith set up a company to market it and develop his ideas further. This company was later to form part of International Business Machines (IBM), one of the largest computer companies in the world. The punched card system has only very recently been replaced by storage of information on magnetic discs.

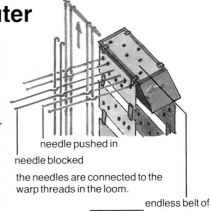

needle pushed in
needle blocked
the needles are connected to the warp threads in the loom.

endless belt of perforated cards

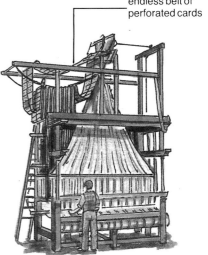

A Jacquard loom (diagram above).

Babbage's punched card.

Magnetic 'floppy' disc.

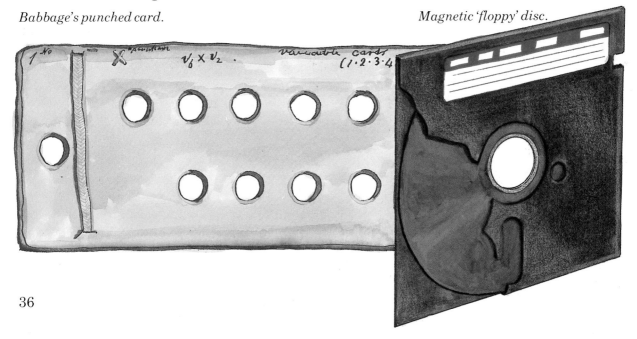

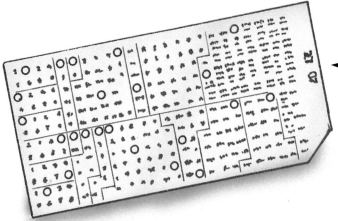

Hollerith's tabulating machine in use, which 'read' the cards.

The biggest boost towards a computer of the type envisaged by Babbage in his 'Analytical Machine', came with the Second World War and the need to break enemy coded messages. Before the war, in 1936, a young German engineer, Conrad Zeus, constructed a mechanical and electrical computer, which he called Z1; it used Boolean algebra, which was a new system of logic, based purely on '1' and '0', the *binary system*. Switches can only be 'on' or 'off'; punched cards either have a hole or do not have a hole in a particular position; so Boole's new algebra was ideal for this purpose. Zeus went on to replace the switches with electrical relays in a new version, the Z2, which was much faster. By the time war came he had produced two even better machines, the Z3 and Z4, but fortunately the Germans did not try to use them for breaking codes. However, in England, research did go ahead rapidly to find a way of interpreting German codes. A machine using relays was produced which could use information at the rate of two thousand characters a second. This was still not fast enough, so a new machine called 'Colossus' was constructed using thermionic valves, which are electronic devices for controlling electric currents. A valve has no moving parts and can operate very much faster than a relay, but it requires a small heating element inside it. Since Colossus contained many thousands of valves, it got very hot and sometimes broke down. Nevertheless, Colossus worked and marked the real beginning of the computer era.

Binary System	
decimal	binary
0	0 0 0 0
1	0 0 0 1
2	0 0 1 0
3	0 0 1 1
4	0 1 0 0
5	0 1 0 1
6	0 1 1 0
7	0 1 1 1
8	1 0 0 0
9	1 0 0 1
10	1 0 1 0
11	1 0 1 1
12	1 1 0 0
13	1 1 0 1
14	1 1 1 0
15	1 1 1 1

Comparison of the binary with the decimal system.

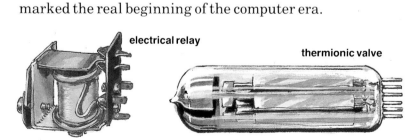

electrical relay

thermionic valve

Although designed for only one type of calculation, Colossus could be *programmed* to do other types but this was not an easy task. Producing a programmable machine was the next big step.

The shrinking computer

In America, before the war, a different approach to computers was being taken. Babbage's design for a versatile machine, able to do any type of calculation, was now at last to be realized. An American, Howard Aiken, studied Babbage's work and decided he could design an up to date version of the 'Analytical Engine'. He obtained financial help from IBM to design and build his 'Automatic Sequence Control Calculator', or ASCC. Switched on in 1943, it was a huge machine. It used electric relays, and was therefore rather slow, but soon better, faster versions were made using valves.

During the war, the need for a machine to work out quickly the trajectory, or path, of a shell prompted work on the Electronic Numerical Integrator and Calculator, or ENIAC. It used valves, so it was very fast, but consumed enormous amounts of electrical power. It could be re-programmed relatively easily, although this was still a fairly laborious job. This drawback was overcome when the mathematician John Von Neumann (who was at that time working on the atom bomb) realized that a program could be stored in the machine in just the same way as the data to be worked on.

These advances were all very well, but the machines were still enormous in every respect. They were expensive to make and expensive to run – and frequently broke down. The invention of the transistor in 1948 was to make a great difference. The transistor does the same job as the valve but is a fraction of the size and does not need a heating element. It uses less power and is very much more reliable. Computers could now be made much smaller and more cheaply. However, they were still too large and too expensive for general use. One reason was that the computer's memory was normally a 'magnetic core': a network of tiny circular magnetic rings, threaded on wires. These cores were bulky and costly to make.

The ENIAC computer, using valves, occupied a large room.

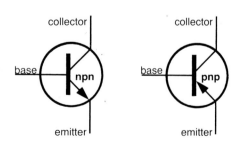

Typical transistor. The three legs are called the base, emitter and collector.

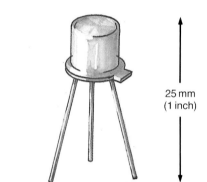

In an npn transistor, current flows from the collector to the emitter and is controlled by a very small current flowing in at the base.

The next push forward came with the space race, and regrettably, the arms race. If spacecraft were to operate successfully then powerful computers were essential. They had to be small, lightweight and reliable. The solution to the problem came with the idea that it was possible to combine most of the components in the electronic circuits into a single component: the *integrated circuit* or 'chip'. It was also possible to make the computer memory in a similar way.

As the method for making these chips improved, so more and more circuitry could be put into them. Eventually, the whole of the central arithmetic part of a computer – called the Central Processing Unit, or CPU – was built into a single integrated circuit. This was the birth of the *microprocessor*.

microchip

An integrated circuit.
Special materials can be deposited on thin slices of silicon (a very cheap material) to make up the components (resistors, transistors, capacitators) required in an electronic circuit. The completed circuit is encased in plastic with the connections protruding as small pins, making it look like a caterpillar. In this way, a circuit containing hundreds of components can be fitted into the space of a few square millimetres.

Inside a space shuttle.
This couldn't operate without micro-electronics.

With the development of this *hardware*, the software, or *program languages*, had also improved. Instructions to the computer could be given in a far simpler way than by having to feed in a series of noughts and ones. Languages like *Pascal*, *FORTRAN* and *COBOL* were developed; *BASIC* is used for most home computers as it uses common English terms.

The way was now open for amazing advances in different computer designs. Speed, reduction in size and power consumption, and cheapness led to the use of computers in almost every area of human activity.

Portable microcomputer.

Computers in the modern world

'Designed by computer' and 'Computer controlled' are now typical catch-phrases of the advertising men. It seems that there is nowhere that the 'hairy caterpillar', the silicon chip, has not now crawled and made its home.

The initial fears that computers would put thousands of people out of work were slow to be realized. The rapid rise of the computer industry at first produced more jobs than were lost through computerization. Now the trend appears to be reversing as integrated circuits are used to control machines, where once skilled craftsmen worked. In many circumstances the carefully controlled machine does the work more accurately and faster – and much more efficiently. In the book 'Resources' in this series, we see that the sources of energy and materials available to man are limited, and that the only way the world can continue into the foreseeable future is to learn to limit their use. The microprocessor has a vital role to play in helping to improve our efficient use of these resources.

It is very expensive and wasteful to build machinery or large civil engineering projects, such as motorways, and then find that they are no good. The use of a *computer model*, that is, a series of mathematical statements which represent the problem or system being studied, helps to minimize this waste. Unfortunately, the hardest part is to make sure that the model is correct. A favourite saying about the computer is, 'Garbage in, garbage out' – if you tell it to do something silly, that is just what it will do. Once the model has been designed, however, engineers can then say to themselves, 'what if . . .', and see how their design stands up when the factors affecting it are changed. This saves a massive amount of re-calculation, and helps to show up any area of weakness in the design.

Using robots on a car production line.

The use of computers that seems to most worry people is in collecting and storing information about individuals in secret files. The National Police Computer at Hendon, in London, is now used to store details about all convicted criminals. However, some people believe it is also used to keep information on those only suspected of committing crimes, and even on people who simply disagree with the political system in Britain or with Government policy. The real worry is that the information in these files may be incorrect; perfectly innocent people may be accused of crimes, or may not be allowed to do certain things because they are thought to be 'enemies of the state'. For this reason, several attempts have been made to have a Freedom of Information Act passed in Parliament, making it possible for everyone to look at their own files.

Computing may now be regarded as a science in its own right, but to mathematicians and scientists, computers are still only sophisticated calculating machines which allow them to push their investigations into the physical world still further. Mathematics did not stop with Gauss, it simply entered a new era, where no single mathematician could hope to be on more than a nodding acquaintance with all the different branches.

However marvellous the progress made with mathematics and computers, it must be remembered that there are still vast areas on Earth where mathematics is meaningless, life is harsh and starvation is a way of life. It is only to be hoped that the integrated circuit developed for exploration of other planets can be used successfully to solve the problems of this one.

Airline pilots and astronauts are trained on simulators. A cockpit, identical to a real one, is built on a computer controlled movable platform. The skills needed can be learnt without ever leaving the ground! Trainees can also be tested to see how they would cope with an emergency, such as engine failure. It is easy to see the savings – especially when a bad mistake is made!

Famine in the midst of plenty!

Time Chart 9000–0 BC

Far East   Middle East   Europe

9000 BC   Stone Age (Neolithic man)

3000 BC   Sumerian City States (Mesopotamia)

Bronze making requires skill in weighing
Sumerians use base 60, have practical skills in geometry
and trignometry

Abacus first used, probably in China

2613–2160 Egypt–Old Kingdom

2500 BC   India–Indus civilization

Egyptians use base 10 number system, unit fractions
invented and Great Pyramids built

2040–1632 Egypt–Middle Kingdom
2000 BC   Crete–Minoan civilization
c.2000–539 Babylonian Empire

Circle of 360 degrees, mathematical tables and
algebraic geometry

1700 China–Shang Dynasty

1567–1069 Egypt–New Kingdom
1500 BC

1000 BC

Magic squares in China

Middle and South American civilizations

524 Buddha

c.600 Greeks seek proofs for mathematical ideas
624–546 Thales, founder of Greek geometry
582–500 Pythagoras proves his theorem and discovers
        irrational numbers
490–430 Zeno tackles the idea of infinite
427–347 Plato founded his Academy and sets new standards
        for proofs

500 BC   Greece–Classical civilization

323–283 Euclid writes 'Elements' on the principles of
        geometry

356–323 Alexander the Great

250 Roman Empire

287–212 Archimedes discovers the laws of flotation and the
        volume of a sphere

220 Great Wall of China built

c.230 Apollonuis studies conic sections

00 BC   Birth of Christ

c.100 Menelaus investigates spherical trigonometry

42

Time Chart AD 300–1700

	Britain / America	Mathematics
AD 300		100–168 Ptolemy's idea that the planets, moon and sun revolve around the Earth begins to spread
		c.300 Diophantus develops algebraic symbols, indeterminate equations and number theory
	391 Library at Alexandria burned	c.400 Decline in Greek mathematics begins
AD 500	476–1453 Byzantine Empire Europe overrun by barbarians	
		622 Expansion of Islamic Empire helps spread new ideas in mathematics
AD 700	Moors (Arabs) conquer Spain	735–804 Alcuin proposes study of the seven liberal arts, including mathematics
	742–814 Charlemagne (France) 849–899 Alfred the Great (first English King)	850 Mahavira sets out rules for multiplying and dividing fractions Hindu number system developed using zero and position value
AD 900		
		967 Gerbert visits Spain and studies the superior Arabic numerals, but not yet accepted in Europe
	1066 Norman conquest of Britain	
AD 1100	1095 First crusade	
	1206 Ghengis Khan invades China 1215 Magna Carta	1170–1250 Leonardo da Pisa investigates negative numbers
	1271–75 Marco Polo's travels in China	
AD 1300	Ottoman Empire (Turkey)	
	Italian Renaissance (14th–16th c)	1465–1526 Scipione Del Ferro finds solution to cubic equations 1473 Copernicus proposes that the Earth revolves around the sun 1545 Cardano writes 'Ars Magna' which sets out rules for negative numbers and proposes imaginary numbers
	1453 Fall of Constantinople 1492 Columbus discovers America	1550–1617 Napier invents his 'bones' and logarithms 1571–1630 Kepler proposes 3 laws of planetary motion
AD 1500	1523 Spanish conquest of South America	1596–1657 Descartes invents Cartesian graphs 1601–65 Fermat studies number theory and proposes his 'last theorem'
	1600 East India Company formed 1620 Pilgrim Fathers. Mayflower voyage 1641–1645 English Civil War	1623–62 Pascal devises a mechanical adding machine, the theory of probability (with Fermat) and his theory on projective geometry 1654 Bissaker develops the slide rule 1646–1716 Leibnitz develops his own system of calculus 1647–1727 Newton defines gravity, sets out laws of motion and develops his own system of calculus
AD 1700		

1700

1707 Act of Union between England and
Scotland to form Great Britain

1707–83 Euler extends use of calculus, studies topology and
introduces mathematical notations and theories

1720

1724 Missionaries expelled from China

1736–1813 Lagrange further develops calculus

1740

"Age of Enlightenment" in Europe
(1694–1778 Voltaire, 1712–78 Rousseau)

1757 British victories in India (Plassey)
1759 and Canada (Quebec)

1760

1768 Cook's first voyage to the Pacific

1776–83 American War of Independence

1777–1855 Gauss works with vectors, incorporates complex
numbers in differential equations, and investigates
the idea of curved space

1780

1788 Colonization of Australia begun
1789 French Revolution

1792–1871 Babbage builds first mechanical computer

1799–1815 Napoleonic Wars

1800

1801 Ceres discovered

1815 Battle of Waterloo

1820

1821 Cauchy brings order to calculus

1840 1837–1901 Victorian Era

Time Chart   1840–1980

1840 Colonization of New Zealand begins

1848 Revolutions in Europe
1848 Californian Gold Rush

1860 1861–65 American Civil War

1870 Franco-Prussian War

1876 Queen Victoria created
        Empress of India
1880

1890 First population census processed by machine, which was
     designed by Hollerith

1900 1899–1902 South African or Boer War

1905 Einstein formulates his 'special theory of relativity'

1916 Einstein's 'general theory of relativity'

1914–18 World War I
1917 Russian Revolution
1920

1929 Wall Street Crash

1936 Zeus builds mechanical/electrical computer, the Z1

1940 1939–45 World War II

Colossus built using valves

1943 Aiken's automatic sequence control calculator built
1903–57 Von Neumann proposes program storage in computers
1948 Transistor developed by Bardeen, Brattaïn and Shockley

1949 Chinese Revolution

1960

1960's Integrated circuits (microchips) developed

1969 First landing on the Moon

1980

45

Glossary

Acceleration – rate of change of velocity.

Algebra – a branch of mathematics in which letters are used instead of numbers.

Analytical geometry – a branch of geometry in which the figures are represented by lines on a graph and therefore by equations.

Base number – the number on which the counting system is based. Our usual system is based on ten.

BASIC – a computer programming language used by most micro-computers – Beginners All Purpose Symbolic Instruction Code.

Binary system – a number system using base two. It is used by computers as the switches they use have only two states – 'on' and 'off'.

COBOL – a computer language specially developed for business use – Common Business Oriented Language.

Complex number – a number made up of a real (ordinary) number and an imaginary number. Used by engineers for solving certain types of equations.

Computer model – a set of equations that represent the way a system (e.g. a motorway network) behaves, which is fed into a computer so that predictions can be made about how the system will work in practice under different conditions.

Conic sections – the set of curves produced when a cone is cut in particular directions.

Co-ordinates – the two numbers which define a particular point on a graph or map. On maps they are normally called a grid reference.

Cosine – of an angle. In a right-angled triangle, it is the ratio of the length of the side adjacent to the angle, to the length of the hypotenuse (the side opposite the right angle).

Cubic equation – an equation in which the variable is cubed (multiplied by itself three times), e.g. $x^3 + 2x^2 + 5x + 2 = 0$.

Data – the information on which a computer performs its calculations.

Decimal point – it is placed to the right of the units column. Numbers to the right of it are tenths of a unit, hundredths and so on.

Differential – a fractional change of a quantity.

Dynamics – the study of the forces which produce motion or movement.

FORTRAN – a computer language used by engineers – FORmula TRANslation.

Geometric algebra – the study of figures and shapes using algebraic notation.

Geometry – the branch of mathematics concerned with the properties of shapes and lines, e.g. triangles, polygons and pyramids.

Hardware – the actual computer and its component parts, as well as associated equipment (peripherals), such as printers.

Harmonic progression – a number series where the denominator increases by a fixed amount, e.g. 1, ½, ⅓, ¼ ...

Imaginary number – the square root of a negative number.

Indeterminate equation – an equation which can have an infinite number of solutions.

Infinite – endless.

Integer – a whole number, such as 1 or 2 or 3, etc.

Integrated circuit – a complete electronic circuit contained on a very small slice of silicon, housed in a small, plastic case.

Irrational number – a number that cannot be expressed exactly as a fraction, e.g. π.

Logarithm – the logarithm (to the base ten) of a number, is the power that ten must be raised to make it equal to that number. The logarithm of 2 is 0.30103, therefore $10^{0.30103} = 2$.

Magnetism – the force of attraction exerted by some materials, like iron and steel.

Mechanics – the study of forces and movement and the behaviour of machinery.

Microprocessor – the main integrated circuit in a computer where the actual calculations are performed.

Negative numbers – a minus number – may represent movement in a direction opposite to a positive direction.

Notation – a series of signs or symbols used to represent quantities or mathematical operations, such as add $(+)$, subtract $(-)$, divide $(\div)$ and multiply $(\times)$.

Pascal – a computer language named in honour of Blaise Pascal.

Position value – in the number 324, each integer represents the number of units, tens or hundreds, depending on its position in the number.

Prime – or prime number, is a number that cannot be divided by any other number except itself or 1, e.g. 2, 3, 5, 7, 11, etc.

Program – a set of instructions given to a computer, telling it how to do the task required.

Program language – the set of instructions used to program a computer. For different applications, e.g. business or scientific, different languages may be used.

Projective geometry – the study of shapes formed when lines are projected through space, such as the shapes of shadows, or the image formed on the film in a camera.

Proof – the series of statements that show the truth of a proposition.

Quadratic equation – an equation in which there is a squared term, but not a cubed or above term, e.g. $x^2 + 3x + 4 = 0$.

Ratio – shows the relative quantities of two or more groups of objects. If a class has twice as many boys as girls, then the ratio of boys to girls is 2:1.

Real number – any number, positive or negative, which can be dealt with in normal algebra – see 'imaginary numbers'.

Reductio ad absurdum – a method of disproving a theory, by showing that the inevitable outcome would be absurd.

Simulator – a device that recreates the controls of a system and their effects, with which the operator has to become familiar.

Sine – of an angle. Ratio of opposite side to hypotenuse (see 'cosine').

Spherical geometry – the study of shapes on and within spheres and other curved surfaces. It is particularly important in the field of global navigation and astronomy.

Squares – the square of a number is the result of multiplying that number by itself, e.g. 3 squared $= 3^2 = 9$.

Square root – of a given number – is the number which when multiplied by itself equals that given number, e.g. 3 is the square root of 9.

Tangent – a straight line which just touches a curved line.

Theorem – an idea or formula that can be proved.

Theoretical – ideas that have been thought out but which may not work in practice.

Theory of Probability – the ideas about the chance of certain events or combinations of events happening.

Topology – a study and description of the general shape of objects even when subjected to continuous distortion.

Trigonometry – the study of the angles of triangles expressed as the ratio of their sides. It is used particularly in navigation and surveying.

Variable – a quantity that can change in an equation. For example, in the equation $y = mx + c$, y and x are variables.

Vector – a quantity, such as a force, which has magnitude or size as well as direction.

Velocity – is similar to speed, but it is a vector, so it is speed in a particular direction; acceleration is a change in velocity, so it may indicate either a change in magnitude of the velocity or a change in direction, such as when going round in a circle.

Index